Yummy Yummy

Yummy Yummy

Layal Kazouh

Dedication

I dedicate this book to Raguel and Uriel, who inspire me daily.

Acknowledgments

I want to thank my mother, Ruth, who never ceases to tell me that I can do it! No matter what "it" is.

About the Author

Layal Elnassis Kazouh was born on December 16th, 1985. She is the mother of two amazing girls, Raguel and Uriel, ages 7 and 4. Layal grew up in Liberia, where she earned her bachelor's of sciences in Zoology from the University of Liberia and continued to earn a master's of Public Health with emphasis on Epidemiology from Cuttington University, also located in Liberia. Layal loves to write, and she found her passion in writing children's books simplifying nature's transaction in stories. Layal is also the founder of a non-profit called the Liberia National Hepatitis Foundation. Fifty percent of the profit from her books goes towards awareness campaigns, vaccinations, and support to prevent and eradicate Hepatitis B from her country of origin, Liberia, where Hepatitis B is endemic and steals lives every day.

The sun came up, shining on a piece of log. A Rollie Pollie made its way to munch on some yummy wood rot in the damp, cool shade of a fallen log.

A Rollie Pollie likes moist places because the moisture helps it to breathe with its gills.

Farther along the edge of the log, in the dark of the shade, a predator watched the Rollie Pollie. But the Rollie Pollie saw the centipede watching it.

"I have 14 legs," the Rollie Pollie thought. "That predator who wants to eat me for breakfast has 30 legs… I better run!"

The centipede dashed forward towards the Rollie Pollie.

The Rollie Pollie rolled into a ball; this is a defense that allows it to be a rounded, tough hard shell this round shape allows it to roll like a tire. It managed to escape the centipede by rolling away quickly!

Rollie Pollie rolled down a hole in the log and slid out the other side. "Weeeee!" Rollie Pollie cheered. "Going down that hole felt like a roller coaster ride." Now he was very far away from the centipede.

"Phew," Rollie Pollie thought. "Not today, predator."

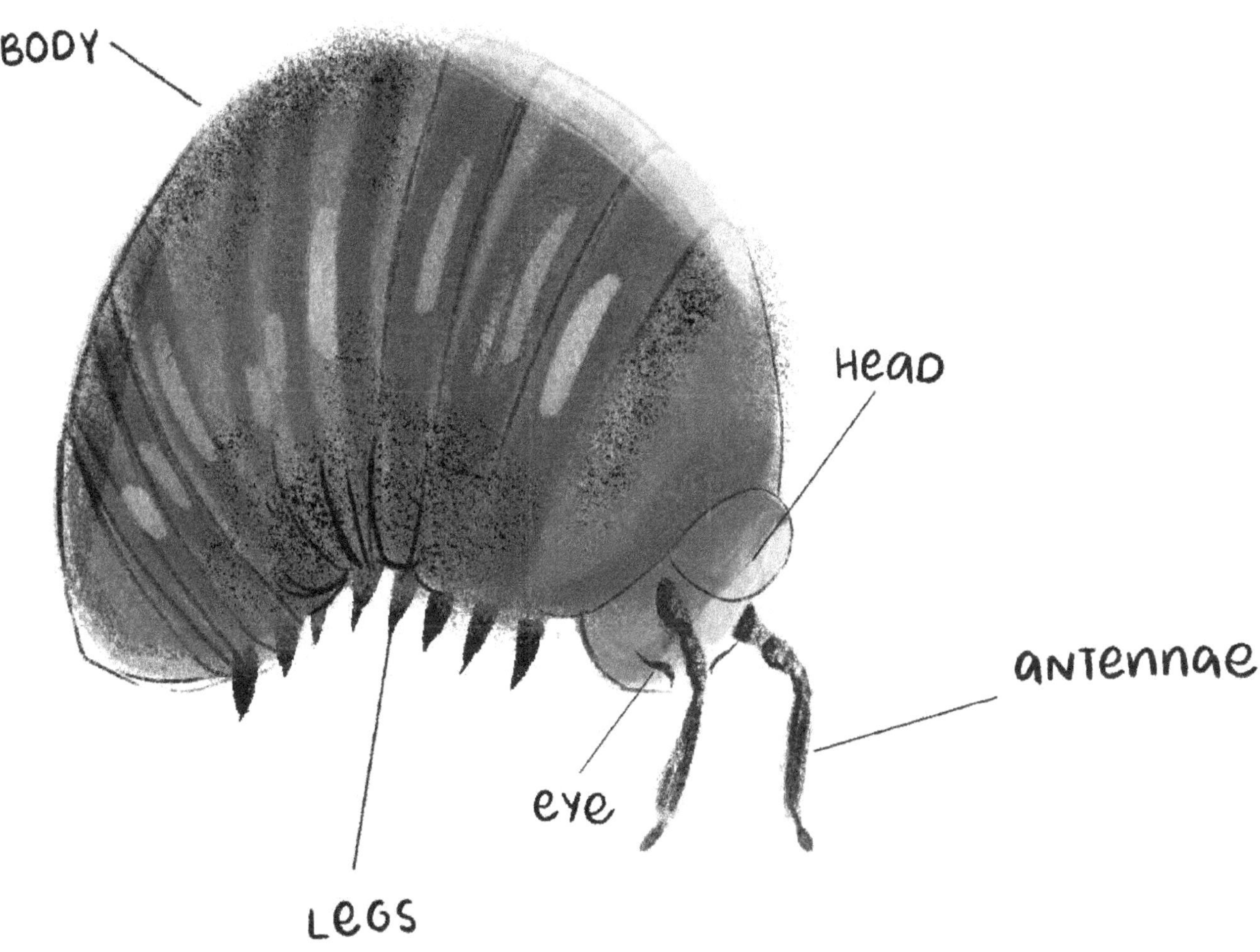

BODY
HEAD
antennae
eye
LEGS

The Centipede did not catch any prey all night, and now the first rays of sunshine were emerging.

Centipedes are nocturnal animals, meaning that they like to hunt and eat at night.

Suddenly, the Centipede saw that yummy, Rollie Pollie. The Centipede was so fast and almost caught it, when he felt a gush of wind that scared him. The Centipede froze in its tracks, and he saw the Rollie Pollie to get away.

The Centipede saw that the breeze had come from the wings of a Carolina Wren. "This is dangerous!" the Centipede thought to himself. "I have to run away from the bird!"

So, the Centipede released the grip of its 30 legs from the log, falling off of the log and quickly crawling under it. The Centipede was safe.

"Ouch! That was painful," the Centipede exclaimed. "Phew," he thought, remembering what just happened. "Not today, predator," and off he went on all 30 aching legs.

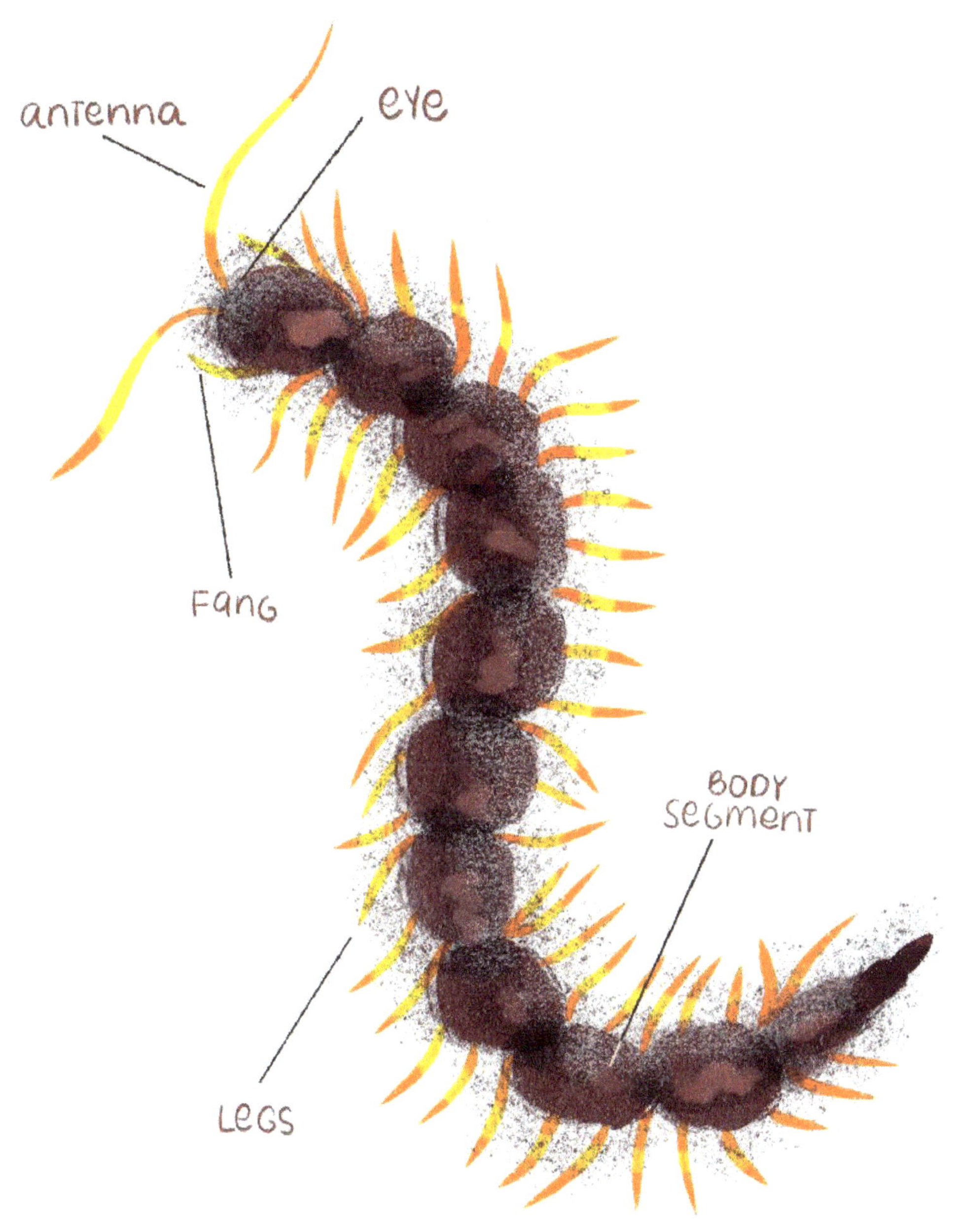

antenna
eye
FanG
BODY SeGMenT
LeGS

The Wren could hear his tummy grumbling. He was so hungry! The movement of a Centipede running so fast caught his eye.

"Two dinners!" he thought to himself. "I can eat the Centipede and the Rollie Pollie—weeee!"

The Wren became very excited. He flew downward quickly to catch its meals, when he heard the loud, grating *cak-cak-cak* of a Cooper's Hawk.

The Wren turned its head to locate the Hawk so that he could flee from it as soon as possible! "Cooper's Hawks are clumsy predators," Wren thought to himself. "I'll quickly fly to the trees."

Off the Wren flew towards a cluster of trees. He could feel the gush of wind blowing from the closeness of the Hawk's wing. The Wren quickly swerved to avoid a tree right ahead of him.

Soon after, he heard a loud thud behind him as he zigzagged through the trees. The When was safely far away. He could see that the Hawk had bumped his head against a tree and had fallen dazed to the forest floor.

"Phew," Wren thought, celebrating his escape. "Not today, predator!"

"Grrrr," he heard the growl of his tummy. Wren still had to find something to eat, but after such a close call with a predator, he chose to rest a little in the safety of the thick foliage.

eye
BILL
TAIL
FEET

A Cooper's Hawk perched still on a log, hoping to blend in with the log with the help of his camouflaging feathers. He felt sure that no one would see him, because the colors of his feathers matched perfectly with the colors of the wood.

He spotted a Carolina Wren bird and wanted to catch it for breakfast. He spread his wings and flew towards it as quickly as he could.

Out of excitement, he began to *cak cak cak* loudly to alert other Hawks that he had spotted it first in case others were around to get his prey.

But suddenly the bird flew through the trees! It flew so fast and began to zig-zagged its way through the trees. Hawk could not catch up.

"This is not good for me!" thought the hawk, "I am going to crash!"

Hawk tried to be careful. He remembered the many times he bumped his head or hit his wings flying through trees.

Suddenly, he lost sight of the Wren! "Did I fly past it without knowing?" he thought to himself. "It has happened before."

He turned to see where it had gone, and a tree appeared out of nowhere! He slammed into it!

"Oh no!" he cried. Now his head hurt, and he was still hungry and there was no Wren in sight. "No breakfast for me," he thought as his tummy grumbled.

BEAK
WINGS
CLAWS
TAIL

What Is a Food Chain?

A food chain looks like this when written on paper. The arrows indicate what prey is eaten by which predator. In the text:

1. The Rollie Pollie eats decaying wood.
2. The Centipede eats the Rollie Pollie.
3. The Wren eats the Centipede.
4. The Hawk eats the Wren.

A written food chain will look like this:

Wood decay ---> Rollie Pollie ---> Centipede ---> Wren ---> Hawk

A food chain is an imaginary link by which one animal hunts another animal for food. It starts with an animal that eats grass or decay in the environment and moves up to larger
animals. It ends with an animal at the top of the food chain that has no natural predators in its environment.

FOOD CHAIN

10